DEVASTATION TO THE HEART

Written and Illustrated By:

Tardanika A. Marshall

Note to Self:

Devastation is the result of severe and overwhelming shock or grief to one's heart and soul. Don't hate yourself over what you have inherited or grow to become; truth be told, everyone has a story.

One woman's devastation to the heart, only makes her stronger.

—T. Marshall

Devastation to the Heart/Marshall

Characters

Mother - Thelma Western

Leroy's Girlfriend - Senica

Father - Leroy Western

Son - La'Darius Western

Son - Jayson Western

Son - Ray Western

(Preacher Boy)

Daughter -Zay'lisha Western

Daughter - Talisha Western

Thelma's Brother - Cole

Thelma's Grandmother - Grandma Lili

Roommate at Hospital - Mrs. Connie Johnson

Grandson - Zaydis Western

Doctor at Hospital - Dr. "P"

Penelope

Urgent Care - Doctor Ellis

Devastation to the Heart/Marshall

    Next Door Neighbor - Mr. Epps

    Neighbor Up the street- Sassy

    Thelma's Dad- Dawayne

TABLE OF CONTENTS

PROLOGUE 1
TWO WEEKS AFTER 3
LEROY 7
HOW WE MET 10
THE LIFE AND EMOTIONS OF THE KIDS 14
TWO WEEKS BEFORE THELMA'S TRAGEDY 21
ABUSE AND THE TRUTH 27

PROLOGUE

Let me give you a breakdown of my family's devastation.

My name is Thelma Western. I am a nurse who is seeking an MD. I have five adult kids, three of whom I haven't heard from in years. Two are still at home—although, we hardly talk, and I can't understand why there is such silence around the house. I also have a grandson named Zaydis Western, who is graduating from high school in a couple of months.

I am married to a man named Leroy Western who I thought was my love for over thirty-five years, but it turned out to be a hoax of a marriage. Lord, why, why, why?

This family hates me, each in their own way; for what their father did to them while growing up. They are causing me to be in distress and I don't know if my heart can take it anymore. Oh Lord, help me; I can't deal.

Two Weeks After

Dr. Penelope comes in and opens the blinds, saying hello to me and my roommate, Mrs. Connie Johnson, a Black female in her late 50's. Mrs. Johnson didn't like that the blinds were opened. We haven't seen the light in a while for having been in a coma.

"Mrs. Western, my name is Dr. Penelope, but they call me Dr. P. May I ask how you are feeling right now? According to my records, you are a survivor ... And Mrs. Johnson, how are you feeling this morning?"

"Mrs. Western, I will be your doctor until we release you, okay? Looking at your record, you are a very strong lady and are pulling through just fine. You will be here for a couple more weeks; not quite there yet but improving. You have been in here for two weeks; do you remember how you ended up in here?"

"What time is it?"

"It's 10:30 a.m," Dr. P. said.

I started crying, "Yes, ma'am. My ex-husband hit me in the head with a metal pole that goes to the fence, and ... um ... kicked me on my side like I owe him something in life."

"Yes, ma'am, you're so right," said Dr. P., looking very upset and startled. I tried to say something, but the doctor got an emergency call.

"I'll be back this afternoon to check on you and talk about your condition some more. Meanwhile, get some more rest and be acquainted with your roommate. Let the nurses know if you need anything."

"Okay, Dr. P," I thought I was the only one in the hospital room.

My neighbor, Connie Johnson, was in here from an overdose of heroin that caused her a heart attack.

"Why you in here?" Mrs. Connie asked me.

"Excuse me; that's not your business. Who are you? That's rude." I responded bluntly.

"No that's not, but oh well ... I'm sorry, excuse me," she stammered, before continuing, "I'll tell you about me ... Due to

Two Weeks After

drug addiction, I had an overdose, which led to heart attack. I was also married to a wonderful man who was a truck driver for over 25 years; one day while driving to Atlanta, he slid on the icy roads and off the bridge. When the autopsy came back, I was told that he had drugs in his system that impaired his functions. It hurt me every day – even talking about it ... I could never have kids. So, to ease my pain, I started taking drugs. It's been six years now, and I've lost everything over these damn drugs, feeling that I had to have it. So, I ended up homeless. I was just trying to talk to you. Sorry, ma'am."

"Okay, I apologize," I said. "Excuse me but I am not the happiest right now. My ex-husband hit me with a metal pole that goes on a fence, kicked me on my side in the middle of the driveway, and spit on me. We have a long driveway. I remember everything ... my head just hurts like hell to move."

"Why the hell did he hit you?" Mrs. Johnson inquired.

"It's complicated. We'll spill the tea ... we have plenty of time on our hands as you can see."

"What the fuck is really going on here?" she uttered out of frustration.

"Well, my ex-husband was on drugs like you, Mrs. Connie,

Two Weeks After

no disrespect."

"None taken, Mrs. Western," Mrs. Connie stated.

"Anyways ..." I said, "Leroy couldn't accept the fact that we were divorced and that his sneaky past caught up with him. So, this is my story and how I got here today."

Two Weeks After

LEROY

First, we have the man I married, the father of all my children—Mr. Leroy Western. He has been a great man to his family until I found out he lived another life and had another personality. The man I knew was a kind, loving man who I thought was my soulmate. While the truth was, he was cheating on me, molesting our kids, and having sex with other women and men in our home. He blames me for everything in life and says that he never loved me; I was "just a cover-up … needed security in a relationship."

My heart dropped.

With a streak of tears coming from each eye … *what the fuck did he just say*?

He never told me about his parents or how his life was as a child. Leroy would always ignore the conversation when his parents' names were mentioned in the conversation.

Leroy's parents were on the way home from a trip and their plane crashed—they died immediately. He lived on his own since the end of his junior year in high school. I was so in love, I never investigated his background or cared much about his family or his past. Maybe, because I didn't have a functional background either, I was blinded by love.

Leroy was diagnosed with schizophrenia, bipolar, and addiction to illegal drugs and prescriptions. All this was due to realizing that he was in love with someone else and wanted a different lifestyle. Leroy thought he was suffering by being with someone he didn't love—me. All these years and he didn't know how to come out with the truth. Now, he hates me and says that he doesn't owe me anything and that he didn't do anything wrong.

Leroy had been raped in the past and 'till this day, has kept that a dark secret—I didn't find out till we got divorced. He never said who did all this to him, but putting this together, led him to do this to his own family. This was all he knew.

Therefore, my kids don't understand that love makes you do crazy things and I can't explain why I stayed here all those years—until now. "All I know is when you're in love with someone that has your heart you tend to do countless things to stay by their side. You start sacrificing the

Leroy

life you had imagined helping their habits and the dreams you thought once were but are no longer, your family comes first. My heart is weighing so heavy on me right now; I can't believe whom I thought was my soulmate, was never. What I thought was a perfect family, was never so.

Leroy

How We Met

It all started during my senior year at Greenbrier high school.

We lived in the country where it's all woods, in a town with a handful of people, where everybody knows everybody. I met this boy named Leroy Western.

He had this certain look about him that made me want to talk to him. I noticed his demeanor was different but never could put my fingers on what it was— I liked him a lot.

Leroy kept passing me in the hallways. Weeks later, he had the nerve to stop me. He stood in front of me and gazed into my eyes. He asked for my phone number and if I'd like to go out that weekend. Lord, I thought I was going to melt. I gave it to him and, of course, I said yes. I was so excited … but I kept that to myself. He kissed me on my cheek and kept walking with his boys. His crew was very popular and well-known. A couple of days later, Leroy called me. He said he was excited about our date that coming weekend.

~*~

Leroy came to get me from my house. I was excited, young, and in love; always ready to go to the movies. As we rode to the theater in the car, enjoying the moment Leroy and I started talking about our future—when we were going to get married and our life goals. It sounded so perfect. The more he talked about the dream I always wanted the more I felt closer to him.

We made it to the movies. About one hour into the film it got boring, so we decided to leave and ride around the town. I had no idea that he was taking me to his cousin's house, where no one was home.

Once there, I found him pouring himself some tequila and me a glass as well. He cut the lights off; we sat down on the couch, smoked a blunt, and watched TV. We kissed and talked and kissed and talked. Then, he started kissing me on my cheek, then my lips before he started rubbing his hands on my arms and legs; one thing led to the next, I was helping him take my clothes off. The next thing I know, we were laying on the couch; we did it.

Ever since that weekend, we hung out a lot. That led to more sex, more feelings—which became stronger—which turned into a relationship where we were inseparable.

It didn't matter to me how my parents felt because they were never there for me anyways. My mom and dad never cared where I was or when I came home because my dad was an alcoholic and a cheater. My mom was always working and claims to have been so tired all the time that she couldn't care for me anymore.

She was sick. She would never tell me what made her so sick, but whatever it was, it kept getting worse and worse. I couldn't stay home.

So, at the age of eighteen was when it all started—life. I started doing what I wanted, feeling that I could find love somewhere else. So, I continued to see Leroy Western. We went to the same college, and a year later, I got my nursing degree, while Leroy got his degree in engineering management.

I still wanted to do more so I enrolled in school again to earn my medical degree. Leroy and I were still together. He had a place in Charleston working as an engineer and he traveled a lot but, he made good money. So, I would come back and forth, to him, for a year. While I was gone, he was seeing *that* man named Carlos. He would always say that was his homeboy and they were like brothers.

I found a job at the hospital working from 5:00 a.m. to 7:00 p.m., off on Sundays, and every other weekend. So, I worked a lot. Leroy worked five days a week, Monday through Thursday, from 10:00 a.m. to 4: 30 p.m., and Fridays at 10:00 a.m. to 2:00 p.m.

Months later, my grandma, who was taking care of my brother, died and she awarded me the house. Months after grandma's burial—still didn't see my mom and dad there—Leroy and I moved into this nice, big 7-bedroom house that I always dreamed of having. I didn't think of getting it this way, all I had to do was take in my brother.

Leroy and I moved in the house, changed it around to our taste, and started our family. Leroy was working on engineering job and trying to start his own company—still making good money. We lived a nice luxurious life, with a gorgeous home and neighborhood. We had goals in life, never wanted for anything, nor did the kids. They seemed happy, I was happy, and life was good—in my eyes anyway.

How We Met

THE LIFE AND EMOTIONS OF THE KIDS

La'Darius

La' Darius, our thirty-year-old, ended up in a car accident which caused him to have a concussion—his mind wanders off and his whole perception of life has changed. Ever since he was about eleven years old, he has not been the same child who lived and wanted a normal life.

He always walked by his father's man cave, where saw his dad having sexual intercourse with men and women, or feeling on another woman while she was making noise. Leroy called him into the room, made him stand in the corner, and said, "It's normal son but you must hush—mom is never to know about this. This is our little secret."

La'Darius nodded his head okay and just stood in the corner quietly looking, throttled by something he never saw before. This kept going on the regular, every day while I would go to work. It was very quiet and peaceful when I was at work. As he got older, he thought what he saw his father do was okay and normal. So, he asked his little sister, Zay'lisha, "Do you want to play around like daddy?"

She said, "Sure," not knowing any better.

Things continued and got serious for La'Darius. He was amazed and still curious. He told her, "No one would understand this or believe you."

She just stared at him and said nervously, "Okay."

Zay'lisha was about ten years old at the time and La'Darius was about seventeen. At that time, she always looked up to her brother, then he started fondling her more and more. Zay'lisha was scared because he threatened her never to tell anyone, or he would kill her in her sleep.

During this time, he also started getting in trouble with the law, not caring about life. La'Darius is now currently living at home with us.

Jayson

Jayson is twenty-five, brilliant, graduated from high school, and loved basketball. Jayson was also awarded a scholarship never thought he would be the one to get rewarded in life. He decided to leave home at the age of eighteen, after his graduation because Jayson was so ashamed of what his dad was doing to him all these years, touching and rubbing on him in ways that weren't normal. Dad made him feel like the only love for him was from men.

Jayson would say, "I always thought that mom would not accept me for what I have become and what dad did to me growing up." Too ashamed to tell everyone that he cared for but didn't care what his father thought of him.

Jay kept that dark secret in his heart for so long, because he didn't want to hurt his mom. So, he left and became a realtor in Atlanta. He was doing very well until the flashbacks came back and he started using drugs. He was missing home but not the bad memories. And he was going through tough nights because of this massive burden that caused him to lose focus on life. I haven't heard from him in years.

Zay'Lisha

Then we have our baby girl Zay'Lisha, twenty-two— a baby having a baby. She used to hang out in the streets a lot, leaving for school but never going. Sometimes, she would be missing in action for days. As time went by, she would disappear for weeks and months, staying with her home girl. She left home, never saying why.

One day, she came home pregnant, not saying who got her like that or why she was very quiet— she hadn't been coming around because she got molested by her dad and her brother.

The Life and Emotions of the Kids

Weeks before she had the baby, she told me that she wanted to come home. When she realized that her dad and La'Darius were still living there, she stayed till she had baby Zaydis, trying to avoid her dad and brother but they kept annoying her. Then, she left again and didn't return for a long time.

She left me with a baby boy named Zaydis Western.

She left because she couldn't figure out how she was going to handle this shit. All she knows is she needs her mom but is too ashamed to come home.

Thinking that her son hates her, she regrets me for not stopping all this bad stuff from happening in the family, yet I still need her. Most of all, how does she tell her mom who the baby daddy is? No one knows about this deep secret that she is holding.

Talisha

I have my other daughter Talisha Western, who is thirty-eight. Talisha never got along with Leroy, and she was the one who saw everything but couldn't do anything about it. She never told me what was going on in the house, because of the fear of her dad and what might happen to them if she told.

Talisha was always observant and said to herself, *Mom may be blind and not know what's going on, but I'll get him one day.* Leroy and she would bump heads all the time, but she would never say anything. He would never bother her on that level; couldn't figure out why. I think their attitudes were very strong and alike.

When Talisha got older she left right after graduation. She never said anything; she packed her clothes, got on a bus, and headed to California to start her life there. She met this man and had a family and became one of the top lawyers at a law firm. As time went by, her boyfriend wanted to get married, and have kids, and she said no. He did not understand why she kept pushing the subject away.

Talisha realized that before she could move on with her life, she had to have closure from her past. It always haunted her, what her father did to her family, and it led her to drinking.

She kept thinking, *is this cycle going to be in me and my family?*

She had these issues to deal with as a woman. We haven't talked in years because she's ashamed of all that had happened and what we all found out, that she should have mentioned it to her. But she feels like since she is a well-known lawyer she can end all the tragedy in her family's life. Talisha's plan is to put dad in jail for what he has done to the family, seek counseling for everyone and get the family back on track and happy so everyone can enjoy life and try to forget the past. Most of all, she

The Life and Emotions of the Kids

began to start having kids with her wonderful husband who wants a family and enjoy life like she is supposed to be.

Ray

Finally, I have Ray—Preacher Boy—who is nineteen, very smart, and loves computers. Ray was the child that always prayed and wanted to play church all the time. He does IT work and is a young preacher striving to have his own church one day.

Ray moved up north, making more money, enjoying life, and is serving the Lord. He was the one I never had to worry about; he always stayed close to me. My son would call or Facetime me every day, since he wasn't welcomed at home.

I think since he was the last one, he took after me. He was the best kid I had. He never gave up on saving his dad or our family. I'm so proud of him. Leroy just keeps ignoring him, treating him like he is the black sheep of the family. My son loves me and is always on my side.

He was the only one who knew my pain as a mother. I cried for many days on my youngest's shoulder. Yet, everyone else faults me and kept me out of the loop.

He left because his dad fucked with him about stupid stuff and forced him to get out if he didn't partake in the family affair. He didn't like the abuse but always wished his father loved him.

Leroy hated and disowned him—I never could understand why.

Two Weeks Before Thelma's Tragedy

My grandson Zaydis is graduating from high school and going into the military at the age of eighteen. This makes me a proud grandmother. Zaydis is the son of Zay'lisha and an unknown father.

"Still searching for the father," Zay'lisha says, then moves on to the next question.

She wasn't comfortable with letting her mom know the truth, so she had left the home only to roam in the street. That made her reluctant to face her mother.

Zaydis wanted graduation and to go away to the Navy dinner; he wanted all his family; aunts, uncles, and his grandad there with him.

I had no clue that the whole crew was going to be there. All were happy to see each other, despite what they had been through while growing up.

Zaydis had no clue to what was going on. I was very happy that all my babies were there at home under one roof eating dinner I had prepared. Yet, no sign of Leroy; nothing unusual with him.

After dinner was over, they got to wrap it up.

I had an announcement, "I am proud to say, y'all, that I am divorced from your father, Leroy Western, as of today. I am no longer with that bastard. Excuse me, you all."

All the children were so happy and laughed and said, "This isn't over yet."

Then, Zay'lisha said, "Yep, you right. I have an announcement to make. Mom, I just want to say I am so sorry for the pain I caused you all these years. I admit that it was so selfish of me; how you took care of me and I never wanted for anything."

"Zay'lisha, what's up? Talk …" I asked her to share.

"I'm sorry for not being in your life," tears running down her face, "I always wanted a son to love, but not like this; so, I just left you. I was childish, but I was a child myself and I just couldn't handle life. I almost ended my life on pills because of what I went through. Now, I have a son who regrets me and doesn't know me, and is graduating from high school. I wasn't there," more tears running down, nearing hyperventilation, "I am so sorry … why this have to happen? But you,

Two Weeks Before Thelma's Tragedy

Zaydis, are the best thing to us since you were born. I know and have always known who your father is. It's out of two men ..."

"Who? Who is he?" With a curious look, Zaydis asks.

"Your dad is ... your uncle La'Darius, or your grandfather." She took a deep breath, heart just pounding, wondering what was about to happen. She looked at me and Zaydis' eyes and face in total shock. Everyone was like, *WHAT*, and *WHEN,* and *WHY* this is just now coming out. It filled the room with pin-drop silence; tears started rolling down Zaydis' face like, *No, he can't be, mom.* He just stood there speechless.

Leroy was invited by Zaydis because it was his graduation dinner and Zaydis is big on family time, but he never knew that this was going to happen. Leroy knocks on the door and Jayson opens it.

Zaydis runs out the door with the car keys and takes off—fast—going 80 down the road thinking and crying. That day Zaydis was upset with everyone in the family, especially his grandad and his uncle because he couldn't believe that they could have done such bad things and that he was still in shock that one of them could be my father. He felt that he had to get far away to clear his head and try to come together for peace to what just happen. Zaydis went to the church parking lot and sat and cried and cried still in shock.

Two Weeks Before Thelma's Tragedy

I ran out to the end of the yard to catch Zaydis, but it was too late he was gone; all I saw was dirt from the car in the air from him driving too fast. As I was looking for him, I saw from the corner of my eye an all-black Chrysler 300 C—the car of Leroy's other lover, the man he left me for. All the kids saw him too, and were in shock, when he said, "Are you ready, baby? Let's get the hell out of here."

All the kids looked at me and I looked back at them like, *what the fuck?* Really, Leroy has completely lost it.

Before Leroy left, he looked me in the face, as he walked toward me, and said, "Why you made your grandson leave?"

I slapped him and said, "Stay the fuck away from my family; I will kill you if you ever come here again. You are the devil! Nothing but the devil. You took our lives and destroyed them, you hurt us all mentally, physically, and emotionally ... you *will* pay for this! You had sex with my daughter, you molested my daughter ... you're a sick fuck! Now, I'm finding out that you may be the father of our grandson ... Then, you allowed my son to engage in such ... sex with her—your daughter—his sister!" When we get this blood test and I find out who the father is, and if it is you, I'm going to kill you. Period.

"Oh, my heart," I punched the shit out of his ass, "You left me for a man!" I walked off saying, "This isn't over."

Two Weeks Before Thelma's Tragedy

As they were walking out the door, La'Darius was cursing Zay'Lisha out for opening her mouth and causing all of this drama. They heard the car door slam and speed off. They came running outside seeing me on the ground, lying there unconscious, with blood everywhere.

Leroy had whipped around, picked up a pole from the ground on the side of the house. He came up behind me and hit me like he was hitting a ball—right across my head, dropping me straight to the ground. When I fell, he kicked me on the side and spit on me. Leroy then ran to the car and left with his boyfriend and backed up speeding out of the driveway.

Leroy was on some pills and had already been drunk before to the house.

The police and ems, not too long after, put an alert out for Leroy; he is now being wanted by the police but nowhere to be found.

~*~

Now, you have Zaydis gone missing, but he got a text while driving around. He was upset, like what he just heard was unreal. The only lady he had loved in his life is in the hospital, unconscious.

Zaydis made it to the hospital and has been by my side every day since. He called his recruiter and explained what happened. As soon as I get out of the hospital, he will be able to report to the military. His

Two Weeks Before Thelma's Tragedy

recruiter understood and was able to delay his departure date until the family got it together.

Meanwhile, I am in the hospital and no one can come up here; no kids but Zaydis. I need rest, so Zaydis goes to the church in the hospital and breaks down. With tears on his face, he falls to his knees, "I'm not a crybaby, but Lord, please help my mom and the tragedies she has encountered. Please, bring her back to me.

Two Weeks Before Thelma's Tragedy

ABUSE AND THE TRUTH

That's when shit hit the fan.

Leroy got laid off because he had been drinking on the job and coming to work late. When I asked him why, he didn't tell me the truth, and said he was stressed about providing for his family. I didn't see how we were in debt.

Leroy insisted that I leave it alone, "No worries," he always said.

I found out I was pregnant with my firstborn, La'Darius, the following day. Leroy was still looking for work when baby boy La'Darius was born. Months later, Leroy found a good engineering manager position in a well-known company. Things, I thought, were coming back together.

~*~

Three years later, my son and his uncle, Cole, went to the mall

Two Weeks Before Thelma's Tragedy

and on their way back they got in a bad car wreck. I thought I was going to lose it, my brother and baby were hurt so badly. "Lord, help me," I prayed.

A car, speeding in the rain, came flying off the interstate ramp and killed my brother instantly. La'Darius survived with brain damage and a mental handicap he will have forever. I noticed something was wrong with him after the accident; he wasn't himself since that day. La'Darius started keeping to himself more or went to the movies. He hated everybody.

As a mom, when my first child, *my* son was not acting like a normal little boy, I was worried. I told Leroy, but he never responded.

I reached out to doctors and they conducted an evaluation on him. Days later, they called us to the office for our baby's results, but Leroy said he couldn't go because he had work to do, even though it was just after hours.

Weeks later, my job told me I couldn't take any more time off; my son was sick, and I didn't know why, so I couldn't focus on anything else. Later that week, I spoke to my supervisor about putting in for a leave of absence without pay. That started hurting me and Leroy's relationship.

On the way home from work, I got a call; it was Dr. Washington from the hospital, saying that he would like to further discuss La'Darius'

Two Weeks Before Thelma's Tragedy

results from the accident. So, I pulled over on the side of the road, the rain was pouring down that day, and I was exhausted. Now, I must hear devastating news about my son, knowing he will never be the same, and that too at such a young age.

The doctor said, "He had a lot of damage to his brain, which caused him to be diagnosed with schizoaffective disorder and bipolar disorder."

"Please doc, tell me what all this means." I know, I'm a nurse, but my mind went blank. Until you been dealt with this card even though you study this its hits you a different way. "Please, help me calm down. It is all new to me," knowing that I have to face the fact that this is not a patient of mine, and that this is my son here we are talking about, and that this situation is life-changing and it will affect all our lives forever. Tears coming down my eyes, as a mother, "This really is heartbreaking."

"Well, yes ma'am; schizoaffective disorder is a mental disorder in which a person experiences a combination of schizophrenia symptoms, such as hallucinations or delusions. This is a disorder that can cause depression or periods of abnormally elevated mood as well, depending on its severity, or whether symptoms of psychosis are present. I know you know all of this but to help you refresh your memory due to you actually being in this situation, I thought I help you out, because

Two Weeks Before Thelma's Tragedy

that's what I'm here for. La'Darius may behave, or feel, abnormally energetic, happy, or irritable. Mrs. Western, he may make poorly thought-out decisions with little regard for the consequences. So, keep a close eye on him, please."

The doctor continued, "This has to be a genetic thing, passed down from you or your husband. Please, call my office and make an appointment so we can see what we can do about getting him some medication and resources for your family."

I cried so hard in the car and waited till the rain let up to get back on the road to head home. I informed Leroy about what the doctor said, but he just ignored me and just walked out. I didn't understand why.

The next day, I called the doctor's office and told them, "My husband and I have to decline the test right now, but please send me resources on how to deal with the disorders La'Darius has."

As I hung up the phone Leroy walked in; already having heard my conversation, he questioned, "Why you on the phone with those people? We don't need any help; don't call them anymore, you understand me? Now, what's for dinner ... I must hurry up and eat because I have a meeting out of town. This is about me opening my own business."

Two Weeks Before Thelma's Tragedy

I kept asking him, "Is this important right now, rushing out of town while your son just got into an accident? It's so fresh and you are leaving, and I never heard you talk about this before … Okay, whatever, bye."

~*~

I had noticed that La'Darius had been following me around the house a lot, crying for me, his head still hurting, and he just needed his mommy's love. I called my neighbor, who lives down the street, to watch La'Darius. She came to the house to watch him till I got back from the doctor. He was sleeping because of the meds so I knew he couldn't do any damage right now and she should be okay watching him for at least thirty minutes or so.

I hadn't been feeling too good myself; caring for other people, I hadn't had time to focus on myself. I got dizzy and that's when I said to myself, *go to the doctor*. I knew I wasn't on any birth control, my breasts were sore, and I had been very sleepy and hungry. I decided to go to the doctor, close to the house. Urgent care was like three blocks away, so I walked, to get some air and think of what was going on in my life and how to fix that and just pray to the one above.

I got there, signed in, and as I about to sit down, a lady I had never met in my life walked up to me and put her hand on my shoulder.

Two Weeks Before Thelma's Tragedy

She said, "My child, I don't know you and you don't know me, but all I'm going to say is … my child, something's not right, but remember … God's got you and just pray about it … oh … and congratulations." She walked out and I never saw her again.

That was such a weird vibe and one of the weirdest moments in my life. Not long after, they called me to the back and escorted me into the room to wait on the doctor.

Finally, the doctor came to the room and introduced herself as Dr. Ash.

"What's going on with you today?" she inquired.

"I am eating too damn much, my breasts are sore, and I have been very sleepy lately." I explained.

"Okay, you might be pregnant but let's see," she laughed.

She took my urine sample and tested positive. I found out that day, I was pregnant with baby number two and I was stunned.

~*~

On the way home, I got a call from my husband asking me, "Why this girl in my house?"

"Her name is Sassy," I told him, "She is watching La'Darius for a minute, I had to …"

"Shut the fuck up and don't let her in my house without my

permission," he slammed the phone down.

Later, at dinner, he came, gave me a hug, and kissed me as if nothing ever happened. After dinner, I told him that I was pregnant with our next child.

"Okay, just don't bring people into my house without me knowing," he put it so bluntly.

I just looked at him and nodded my head. Life kept going on as usual facing life's obstacles and preparing for the next baby in my life. M

~*~

Then baby number three, four, and five came. Every time we would make up, another baby came—we had a football team in four years.

After our fifth baby, Leroy really began acting stupid. He would go MIA a lot, come home when he was ready, and would only be home when I was at work. He would always have excuses to leave, never helping around the house like he used to, or go out with me unlike before. I wish I had known why he didn't want to go out with me anymore.

After a while, Leroy stopped paying bills and coming home. Although, he was quick to watch our bank account—we had over sixty thousand dollars in there. My heart dropped when he withdrew thirty of

Two Weeks Before Thelma's Tragedy

it. I never knew if he was still working, because he stopped talking to me about everything.

I was fine because I had a part time nursing job and all the money in the bank, but I was getting nervous, knowing we had to raise our kids and live. That was our savings we started when we got married. We said we wouldn't touch it without the other's consent.

I needed to know what the hell he spent thirty thousand dollars on, when we had everything we could ask for. Not consulting with me on this … hell no … Now, I was fed up.

As the days went by, Leroy would go to the bank and get more money as if it was all his. But me … my dumb ass overlooked it and stayed by his side, hoping he had a good reason to take the money from our accounts, and that he still loved me. Blinded by love; makes you think crazy.

~*~

I got a call from my dad who lives in Vegas with some woman now and he told me that the reason he left my mom after I graduated was that she was so sick; he said she was holding him back in life. Another man had given her HIV, and that's why she was sick and hurting all those years.

I kind of felt that something was going to happen soon. It was hot, like eighty-five outside, and I felt this big, cold air wave came across me, as I walked to the house from the mailbox. I got the mail and it was addressed to me. Since it was a long walk back to the house, I decided to read the letter.

The letter she wrote me, read:

Dear Thelma,

My precious daughter whom I only wanted the best for and whom I see that will have a successful career. I am writing this letter to explain what happened between me and your father because I know you blame him for all the wrong in this relationship and why it tore our family apart.

The truth is that your dad was a wonderful father who loved me and only me, but I was the one that kept going behind his back messing around with other men, and he still stayed until one day I messed around with this one man that was well-known in the streets that I felt that I had to have, like they say be careful of what you ask for, you shall get it not the way you wanted or get more of what you bargained for. So, we had sex then months later. I found out that this man died of what he had, and he gave it to me, but he caught it from needles, and I caught it from sex and that's why our relationship ended.

Your dad knew of him and stayed clear of me and told me to get checked out because of what he knew about this man. I then became HIV positive and he couldn't take it anymore and deal with the fact that I betrayed him and tore our family apart, so your dad left. I then started getting sicker and had to take a lot of medication. As you and your brother got older, I couldn't take care of you or be the mother I needed to be, so that's when I decided to send your brother to your grandma's house for her to raise him. You were too old for me to send you off, I prayed and hope good would come to you and you wouldn't follow my footsteps.

Your dad then started talking to another woman and moved out after you left. Please, don't hate him because he is not the cause of our family falling apart. I was the one who did run the streets. I wasn't able to be saved I ran the streets my whole life, and my parents tried to save me, but I didn't listen.

Your grandma said to me that she would always be there for me when I'm ready, but she couldn't help me. I had to want to help myself, but by the time I realized how important life was to me, it was too late. I love you, your brother, and your father. May God look over y'all.

I'm am on my deathbed crying for peace and hope you never bear what I went through in life. I will always be there for you and look over you from heaven. Please, don't fault your dad, because it wasn't his fault that I ended up this way. I was fast all my life."

Love, Mom

Two Weeks Before Thelma's Tragedy

After I read the letter, I just fell to the ground and cried. I didn't want to believe my dad, but he was right all this time.

I was missing my mom and wanted her back, but she was too sick to call and talk to me, so I just didn't bother her. I'm glad I got clarification on what was actually going on. I only talked to her a couple of times since I left home. She couldn't make it to Cole's funeral because she was sick and embarrassed of herself and didn't want anybody questioning her.

I found out that dad was a good, hardworking man who loved his family. I didn't know this, but dad said I never wanted to hear the truth, so he left and kept that to himself all these years. I wish I knew, I would have never left home. I would have stayed with my mom and dad. I wish I could go back and change a couple of things, so I could have been there for my mom in her time of need. Now, I think to myself that I was very selfish growing up. I only cared about me being happy, not understanding what grownups go through after they are out their own, with families, trying to make it.

~*~

Leroy asked me why I kept crying. I told him that my mom died and we all must go, as a family, up north. He said okay and we packed up and flew to New Jersey. We acted like a family and played like we were the perfect couple. The kids, I noticed, would start acting weird. They were so quiet around their dad. You could hear a pin drop whenever he was around. I kept thinking to myself, *what's wrong with my kids; this is not normal.*

I had a talk with my dad, after the funeral. I couldn't do anything but hug him and apologized for how disrespectful I'd been toward him all these years. Not knowing the truth, thinking that it was him that caused this tragedy, but it wasn't him. He was just trying to be a good husband and father—it was mom, damn.

Dad said he was sorry for not telling us and not reaching out. He thought we were disowning him since we left; I mean his own son hated his guts and died not knowing the truth about his mom and dad.

Dawayne cried, "You're my kids … why would you think that I would want you to go and leave me? Not a day went by that I don't regret the past - I just couldn't say nothing, I didn't want you to see the truth, so, I just took the blame for everything all these years."

We made amends and hugged it out. I have closure now and have my father back in my life. He now will be able to see his grands grow up and be the grandfather he always wanted to be. He was so happy to see all five of my kids— laughing, and not expecting me to have all these kids,

Two Weeks Before Thelma's Tragedy

but happy. I felt better and could move on from my family issues.

I also met the crazy girlfriend of his, she seemed nice, very bubbly, and happy all the time—been around her the whole week and she is just so, so happy, like she needs to calm down. But that's what he likes. Let him be happy. Although he told me that he was ready to leave her, she was just keeping his mind off his kids and life, in general. They currently live in Vegas, but he is ready to leave the busy lifestyle he has had since he left mom. He is retired and I thought about him moving in with us. Leroy acted funny about it, so I needed to sit down with him and have a talk.

Weeks later, I spoke to Leroy about dad moving in. Of course, as soon as I said, "My dad is coming to stay with us," he stopped me in the middle of my sentence, like he always does, cutting me off.

He said, "We don't need anyone in this house. No."

"But Leroy, you're never here and you always have to go to meetings or out of town. You don't think that dad would be a great candidate to help with the kids, and me going back to work since 'you're gone half the time? I think it would be great."

Leroy responded with a loud affirmative voice, "I said, NO," as he walked away and went into his man cave.

I had never been in that room since we moved into the house. He was either in the man cave or gone.

Two Weeks Before Thelma's Tragedy

The job I wanted called and offered me a position, weekends only, so I took it since the kids were older and could stay home and watch each other. When I got home from the grocery store, I made the announcement, "I have a full-time job on weekends only, so, dad will be watching y'all, while I'm at work."

Zay'lisha said, "No, mom; please, don't leave us."

I knew how Leroy could be so mean to them, but I didn't think too deep about other things going on. As a mom, who would think of negative things being done by someone you love.

"Zay'lisha be a big girl; daddy loves y'all, so be nice."

Jayson just sat there with his head down.

Leroy said, "Good baby, I can spend more time with the kids."

"Well, you'll start this Friday night." It was Wednesday at that time.

I never returned to the last job because Leroy would go missing too much. Now that the kids are a little older, we can try this again.

When Leroy and I were getting ready for bed, he said, "We are going to be fine, and things are getting back right."

And looked at him like, *okay*.

Love will make you say yes to shit that doesn't feel right at that moment. I was too intimidated by him, to ask the questions that had

Two Weeks Before Thelma's Tragedy

been on my mind for a couple of months. I needed closure too—*where are you at every other night, or why are you taking money out of the account, and for what?* But I kept that to myself thinking, today was not that day.

~*~

When that day arrived, the shit started hitting the fan. I had been working for a month and loved the job—they asked me to do more days a week. Leroy agreed to be home when I had to go to work.

The kids would get called into the man cave every other day or when I had to go to work. He would start changing his schedule around just to do sick shit. . If he wasn't messing with them in an uncomfortable way, he would have people—his toys— coming in through this side door when he was ready to play around—men, women, it didn't matter. He *loved* everybody.

He called Talisha in, but she refused to obey what he said, so he would just beat or slap her. Then, he would turn around and hug her and say, "I love you Talisha," before moving on to the next child. By midnight, when I came home, they would all be in bed together, asleep, waiting on me to open the bedroom door to tell them I was home, and I loved them. They would get up and go to their rooms, as if Leroy was a stranger in the house. They felt at ease and at peace, knowing their dad couldn't bother them anymore that night.

One Saturday night, the neighbor heard some noise coming from the house. He wanted to be nosy, and check things out, because he knew my schedule and, from time-to-time, he would go over to check out the house. Tonight, something didn't seem right, and he walked toward the back door, near the man cave room. The flood-lights came on, scaring him. Leroy popped his head out of the window, trying to see what set the lights off, but couldn't see anything.

Mr. Epps was on the side of the house in the dark spot where no one could see him. Leroy went back to doing what he was doing, and Mr. Epps peeked in the corner window. He was shocked and appalled by what saw. He left.

You would never know anyone was at the house because everyone who came over take an Uber, so no cars were in the driveway but Leroy's. Mr. Epps went walking the next day and started keeping track of what he was seeing.

Leroy caught him one night, by creeping up on him—he felt someone, or something, was prowling around his man cave. He threatened Mr. Epps, "If you tell anyone what I am doing, I will come to your house and personally kill you or make you my bitch," he laughed, "Or, I might even make a false report that you are the one doing it to my

Two Weeks Before Thelma's Tragedy

kids."

Mr. Epps never told anyone to this day what he saw, but he was very concerned and worried about me, the kids, and our well-being. So, he stepped back for a while and just observed, so he could collect evidence on Leroy's ass, to give to me; otherwise, I wouldn't have believed him. Leroy had enough; he decided to leave and never come back. He got what he needed from me, wiped the joint account clean, and built his empire elsewhere. He fell in love with Senica and I haven't heard from him since I got hit in the head with the pole from the fence.

~*~

After I finally got out of the hospital and was released to my grandson Zaydis, we went home to a dinner that Talisha and Zay'lisha had put together—I heard it was spaghetti, fried chicken, and salad—right up my ally. I was so hungry, tired of all that hospital food. I had lost a lot of weight. So, I really I needed some good food.

I mentioned to Zaydis, "Everyone is meeting us at the house, so take your time driving us home so we can have a talk and I can hear what's on my grandson's mind."

"Grandma," Zaydis says, "Don't worry about nothing now. You just got out of the hospital.

I said, "Boy, shut the fuck up and talk to me about what's in your

Two Weeks Before Thelma's Tragedy

heart right now. I'm grandma, no matter how I feel. Boy, you are my priority and will always be my priority, understand? I love you, Zaydis." With tears rolling down from my eyes.

"I love you too; and yes, grandma, I do understand." He gave her a kiss on the cheek at the light.

So, I asked, "How do you feel about all of this? Because you are the one that matters, grandson."

Zaydis said, "I feel very confused and upset with my mom and I hate my uncle La'Darius and my grandad," Zaydis adored them growing up. "I never want to see or hear about the bad things they did to the others."

Leroy never showed anything around Zaydis, I guess he had this feeling in him, *don't touch him*.

He said, "Grandma, I just didn't know how to cope with so much news in one sentence. It still hurts and I can't wait to leave this Friday. I don't think I'll be back. I will send for you, grandma. When I find out tonight …"

"Oh, the results are back, yes, that's one reason Talisha wanted us to have dinner."

"She thinks it's time we get some answers and put this in our past so that we can have closure."

Two Weeks Before Thelma's Tragedy

"Okay, yes, it is."

When we finally got to the house and all the kids say, "Surprise!" That was one of the most heartfelt things that I had felt in a long time from this family. They had a gift, a welcome home banner. I got hugs too—from all my five kids. They sat down by the couch, where I was laying, because I was still on bed rest, so we decided to eat in the den area.

They all cleaned up, then sat down again.

Talisha said, "Okay, this is the day that we all need to release what is going on in our past lives and is hurting us now. First, we going to start with who is the father of Zaydis, and I have the results right here … The birth father of Zaydis Western is … La'Darius Western, with 99.99% proof of him being the father."

La'Darius got up.

I yelled in a voice no one had ever heard from their mother, "La'Darius Western, you better sit your ass down, right the fuck now. You will face this battle, your nasty fuck of a son … But now, I'm going to calm down, and we—as a family—are going to figure this shit out because I am still your mom at the end of the day."

On the inside, I wanted to break down and cry so badly because I couldn't believe what I just heard about him being Zaydis's father.

Two Weeks Before Thelma's Tragedy

"La'Darius, how did this all come about?"

"I don't want to say, because it's serious, mom."

"No. Spill it, La'Darius."

"Okay. Dad molested me since I was about 7 years old."

All the kids started talking at one time. We all went through something with dad in some type of way he affected all of us.

"Well, what about you, Talisha? What about you, Ray? Did he do that to you too?"

"Talisha and Ray said no, dad hated us because he couldn't intimidate us as he did them. He tried both of us one time, but I didn't see how that was right. So, I would literally hide under the sink so he couldn't find me, all the way till you would get home. I would set my watch for ten minutes before you walk through that door, because dad's attitude and demeanor would change once you came home. He didn't want anyone, especially you, to know that he lived this other life."

"Dad would have multiple men and women in his man cave room. He would make us walk in a line, quietly back to our rooms, and threaten us not to speak about this to no one. He would always say, 'No one will believe you anyway.'

"'It's okay to do this,' that's what La'Darius said dad would say."

"He would have sexual intercourse, oral, in front of all of us. And

Two Weeks Before Thelma's Tragedy

he would call us into the room, one-by-one, and make us take our clothes off to perform oral sex on him …"

As the kids talked, Zay'lisha threw up. She couldn't take it anymore. She felt such a heavy weight on her, she just sat there with tears coming down her face, shaking, as if to say, *if someone had only helped me when I cried, but no one understood me.*

Mumbling, "I'm so sorry, Zaydis … I'm so sorry, mom …" repeatedly, as if deep down, she thought it was her fault.

My face was red, and I was in shock.

"La'Darius said, 'dad told me to do it to my sister and don't tell anyone' and that, 'it was okay.'"

I looked at La'Darius and saw tears rolling, one-by-one, down his left cheek.

"All we knew was what he taught us. We were mad at you because you didn't see us crying out in many ways. I felt that you were blinded."

"Ray said that's why we all left and took different paths in life. We tried to do better, knowing we were facing our past lives. We tried to do better and remember how not to be if we had kids."

Zaydis manned up and apologize to his uncle—his daddy—that he understood him and respected that. "This wasn't my mom's nor my dad's fault."

They hugged.

He hugged his mom and looked her in her face and said, "This is the tie that we need to start over, this is a new chapter, but always remember grandma is my number one mom."

"I understand," said Zay'lisha.

Ray recommended that we all get counseling after we figure what to do about dad. Before we could continue talking, there was a ring at the door.

Mr. Epps, the neighbor, noticed that Leroy's was never there anymore and it looked safe to come and tell me the news.

"Hello, everyone. Mrs. Thelma, are you okay? I have been worried about you since you went to the hospital. But I had to do some digging to have all of us safe from that horrible, sick individual of a man."

"May I ask to whom you are referring?" said Thelma and Talisha, in unison.

"Your father, Leroy. It's so important that you all need to hear this. This involves the kids too."

"Yes, come in, and let's talk about this with the kids."

Mr. Epps had a recording of what he saw in the window. That's

Two Weeks Before Thelma's Tragedy

why he never said anything else after Leroy threatened him in so many ways.

Mr. Epps told us, "I knew the man that he was seeing all these years, because he was cheating with that man and they were living another life together. His name is Senica and they stay two towns over. I was messing around with Senica about 7 years ago. He has HIV that's why I stopped talking to him, and he was very abusive to him. They built a house on 15 acres of land and got two cars. They started a company in Atlanta, doing engineering work—a company that works with technology, developing different ways to upgrade computers. Leroy then comes home and lives this life, with his wife and kids. Sick. Molesting his kids is sick …"

"… What are we going to do about this about this, Thelma?"

I told the kids, "The plan is going to be that we will all meet here tomorrow at 3:00 p.m. We are going to confront your dad and call the police, because he is not going to destroy my family and think that he can get away with it. Zaydis, call your grandfather as if you need to talk to him, and get him over here."

Zaydis made the phone call to Leroy, while I was on the phone with the investigator telling them what time to arrive.

~*~

Two Weeks Before Thelma's Tragedy

The next day, Leroy decided to get wasted and pop some pills before coming to see me and the kids. He was already ashamed of what he had done all those years. He felt the nervousness in his body and coldness in his soul. He still had hatred in him, and his plans were different from their plans.

Leroy's boyfriend told him, "Slow down, you're driving too fast! Why do I need to get into the family mess you created? You should have just ended this shit a long time ago. Damn … now look at what we are dealing with. I'm nervous for you, I feel something's not right … Slow down Leroy, please."

They make it to my house and before Leroy got out of the car, he takes his pistol out of the armrest console, slightly sliding it into his back pocket, where no one could see it as he got out of the car. He walked in the door, staggering, leaning, and starts crying.

All the kids, grandkids, and I were in the front room together, standing around Leroy, as he said he was sorry for what he did and told us about his past that no one knew about.

He came out with, "I contracted HIV from someone …"

Senica stopped him, "You got HIV from me."

Leroy said, laughing, "I can't believe this after all these years, why didn't you tell me? Why now, Senica?"

Two Weeks Before Thelma's Tragedy

"Shit, this is the time"

Leroy looked at Senica and took a swallow of his tequila, "Back to you later, Bitch …"

"I was saying … I got molested when I was a little boy and was told it's okay. That's all I knew …" He continued explaining, "I'm really fucked up …"

As he was saying the last sentence, he pulled out his pistol and started swinging it around. "My baby girls, daddy is sorry, and I love you all …"
Everyone's hearts were beating fast.

"Please, put that gun down …"

He has it swinging every way, then the lights go out …

To be continued …

Two Weeks Before Thelma's Tragedy

www.ingramcontent.com/pod-product-compliance
Lightning Source LLC
LaVergne TN
LVHW081525060526
838200LV00044B/2005